HO
JOKES
FOR COOL KIDS!

HOT JOKES FOR COOL KIDS!

Buster Books

Compiled and edited by Chris Maynard
Designed by Zoe Quayle
Cover illustration by Martin Chatterton

First published in Great Britain
in 2004 by Buster Books, an imprint
of Michael O'Mara Books Limited,
9 Lion Yard, Tremadoc Road,
London SW4 7NQ

A CIP catalogue record for this book is
available from the British Library.

ISBN 1-904613-33-0

3 5 7 9 10 8 6 4 2

Visit our website at
www.mombooks.com/busterbooks

Printed and bound by Bookmarque Ltd, UK

CONTENTS

6 SCHOOL HOWLERS

16 COMPUTING CRAZY

22 DUMB DOCTORS

29 KRAZY KIDS

35 ANIMAL CRACKERS

49 MONSTROUS MIRTH

60 KNOCK, KNOCK

70 JUST DUMB!

84 INSULTS

96 OVER TO YOU

School Howlers

Mother: What did you learn in school today?

Son: How to write.

Mother: What did you write?

Son: I don't know – they haven't taught us how to read yet.

Teacher: It's very rude to reach over the table for cakes. Haven't you got a tongue in your head?

Pupil: Yes, but my arms are longer.

Teacher: Sarah, what was the first thing King James did on coming to the throne?

Sarah: Sit down?

EXCUSES, EXCUSES...

I haven't done my homework because...

...my pet gerbils had babies,
and they
used it to make a nest.

...I didn't want the other kids
in the class to look bad.

...I didn't want to add to your
already heavy workload.

...I was at a rally last night demanding
better pay and conditions for our
hardworking teachers.

...I was being followed on the way to school
by spies so I had to eat it to avoid it
falling into enemy hands.

...my dog ate it, then my
science project ate my dog.

Mother: Freddie, why don't you want to go back to school today?

Freddie: Well, I can't read, I can't write and my teacher won't let me talk.

Mother: George, why does your geography exam have a big zero over it?

George: It's not a zero, Mum. The teacher ran out of stars, so she gave me a moon instead.

Teacher: Didn't I tell you to stand at the end of the line?

Bobby: I tried, but there was someone already there.

Teacher: Jackie, if you subtract 932 from 1,439, what is the difference?

Jackie: That's what I say, what's the difference?

Teacher: If I had seven oranges in one hand and eight oranges in the other, what would I have, Joe?

Joe: Big hands.

Teacher: Ralph, your essay on 'My Dog' is exactly the same as your brother's. Did you copy his?

Ralph: No, teacher, it's the same dog.

Teacher: Which family does the octopus belong to?

Robert: Nobody I know.

Teacher: What would happen if you took the school bus home?

Joe: The police would make you bring it back.

Teacher: If your father gave your mother ten chocolates and then took nine away, what would your mother get?

Sandy: Angry!

Dad: I'm worried about you being at the bottom of the class, son.

Son: But Dad, they teach the same stuff at both ends.

Teacher: What do we call the outer layer of a tree, Billy?

Billy: I don't know, Miss.

Teacher: Bark, silly, bark.

Billy: Woof, woof!

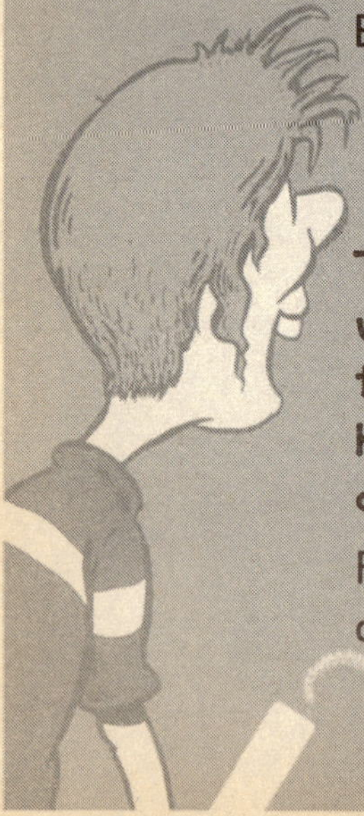

Teacher: Fred, I told you to write this poem out ten times to improve your terrible handwriting, and you've only done it seven times!

Fred: Sorry, Sir. It looks like my counting isn't too good either.

The class was out of control.
'OK, all the idiots please stand up,' said the sarcastic teacher. After a long silence, one girl rose to her feet.
'Now then, Mary, why do you consider yourself an idiot?' enquired the teacher with a sneer.
'Well, actually I don't,' said Mary, 'but I hate to see you standing up there all by yourself.'

Father: What did you learn in school today, Son?

Son: That three plus three is seven.

Father: But three plus three is six.

Son: I guess I didn't learn anything today then.

Teacher: Jane, do you know what time we start school here in the morning?

Jane: No, teacher, I don't. I've never been here for that.

Teacher: John, you've been late for school every day this week.

John: No, teacher, I was only late for school four days this week. The other day I was absent.

Teacher: Rachael, you've been late for school five days this week. Does that make you happy?

Rachael: Sure does, that means it's Friday.

Teacher: Do you know what the word 'tardy' means?

Sam: No, Sir, I don't. You must have covered that before I got here.

Teacher: John, how would you like it if I were ten minutes late for school every morning like you are?

John: It would be great. We could ride to school together.

Teacher: You've been ten minutes late for school every day this year and all you do is come up with stupid excuses.

Frankie: I know. If I could be fifteen minutes late, that would give me enough time to come up with better excuses.

Computing Crazy

What do you call a computer in a raincoat?

Mac.

How do you stop your laptop's batteries from running out?
Hide their shoes.
Who holds up stagecoaches and steals computers?
Click Turpin.

Do you like web jokes?

Yes, they're e-larious.

Why couldn't the apple send an e-mail to the orange?

Because the lime was engaged.

Who is the most popular wizard on the Internet?
Harr e-Potter.
Have you seen the baked bean website?
No, I've only just got wind of it.

Why did the chicken cross the web?

To get to the other site.

How do wizards turn on their computers?

They press the on/off witch.

Doctor, Doctor, I feel like I'm part of the Internet.
Well, you *do* look a site.
Why is this the last Internet joke?
Because everyone has had e-nough.

Dumb Doctors

Doctor, Doctor, you've taken out my tonsils, my adenoids, my gall bladder, my varicose veins and my appendix, but I still don't feel good.

That's enough out of you.

Doctor, Doctor, I keep thinking I'm a frog!

So what's wrong with that?

I think I'm going to croak!

Doctor, there is a man in the waiting room with a glass eye named Brown.

Wow, what does he call his other eye?

A man walks into his doctor's surgery. He has a cucumber up his nose, a carrot in his left ear and a banana in his right ear. 'What's the matter with me?' the man asks the doctor. 'Well', the doctor replies, 'it's quite clear you're not eating properly.'

Doctor, Doctor, my baby's swallowed a bullet.

OK, just don't point him at anyone until I get there.

Doctor, Doctor, what did the x-ray of my head show?

Nothing at all.

Doctor, Doctor, I feel like a burglar.

Well, have you taken anything for it?

Doctor: I'm afraid you need glasses.

Patient: How do you know?

Doctor: I could tell when you came in through the window.

Doctor, Doctor, I feel like I'm disappearing.

Yes, I can see you're not all there.

Doctor, Doctor, you have to help me out.

Certainly. Now, which way did you come in?

Doctor, Doctor, something is wrong. I can't feel my legs.

Yes, I'm afraid we've had to amputate both your arms.

Doctor, Doctor, I'm turning invisible.

Sorry, I can't see you now.

Doctor, Doctor, I really want to paint myself in gold all over.

Don't worry, it's just a gilt complex.

Doctor, Doctor, I've just been bitten on the leg by a werewolf.

Did you put anything on it?

No, he seemed to like it just as it was.

Doctor, Doctor, I keep thinking I'm a python.

You can't get round me like that, you know.

[On the telephone]
Doctor, Doctor, my wife is pregnant, and her contractions are only two minutes apart!

Is this her first child?

Of course not, you idiot, this is her husband.

A man goes to his doctor for a check-up, because he's been feeling a little ill. After the check-up the doctor comes out with the results of the examination.
'I'm afraid I have some bad news. You're dying and you don't have much time,' the doctor says.
'Oh no, that's terrible! How much time do I have?' the man asks.
'10...' says the doctor.
'10? 10 what? Months? Weeks? What?' he asks desperately.
'10...9...8...7...'

KRAZY KIDS

As he was walking along the street, a priest saw a little boy trying to reach a high door knocker.

Anxious to help, he went over to the boy. 'Let me do it, Son,' he said, rapping the knocker vigorously.

'Great,' said the little boy. 'Now, run!'

Billy: How did Darth Vader know what Luke Skywalker was getting for Christmas?

Sally: I don't know, how?

Billy: He felt his presents.

Young girl: I would like to buy a bundle of hay, please.

Farmer: Is it for *your father?*

Young girl: Of course not, it's for the horses.

Teacher: Who was the first woman on earth?

Angela: I don't know.

Teacher: Come on, Angela. It has something to do with an apple.

Angela: Granny Smith?

What did the boy flea say to his girlfriend?

I love you aw-flea.

A boy made a wooden car with a wooden engine, wooden tyres and wooden seats.

Guess what?

It wooden go.

What did the lawyer name his daughter?

Sue.

What did the Eskimo boy say to the Eskimo girl?

What's an ice girl like you doing in a place like this?

What's green, round and goes camping?

A boy sprout.

Josie: I think my brother was born upside down.

Anne: Why?

Josie: Well, his nose runs and his feet smell.

Did you hear about the boy who couldn't get to grips with decimals?

He couldn't see the point.

Laura: You remind me of the ocean.

George: Romantic, wild, untamed and restless?

Laura: No, you make me sick.

What's the wife of a hippy called?

Mississippi.

Animal Crackers

What burger does a horse eat?

A double clopper meal.

Little girl: Grandpa, are you a frog?

Grandpa: No, why do you ask?

Little girl: Well, Dad said we'll get your house when you croak.

What is the difference between a fish and a piano?

You can't tuna fish.

What did the beaver say to the tree?

It's been nice gnawing you.

How do you catch a unique rabbit?

Unique up on him.

How do you catch a tame rabbit?

The tame way.

Why do sharks only swim in salt water?

Because pepper water makes them sneeze.

MOVIE MADNESS

A man goes into a cinema with his dog. The film is a comedy, and when there's a funny scene the dog starts laughing. Later there's a sad part and, sure enough, the dog starts crying. This goes on throughout the whole film, with the dog laughing and crying in all the right places.

A man sitting a few rows back has seen the whole thing and decides to follow the man out. In the street, he approaches the dog owner and says, 'That's truly amazing.'

'It certainly is,' the dog owner replies. 'He really hated the book.'

Which cat discovered America?

Christofurry Columbus.

What should you do if you find a snake in your bed?

Sleep in the wardrobe.

What fast food do sharks eat ?

Clamburgers.

What do you get when you run over a budgie with a lawnmower?

Shredded Tweat.

Shhhhhh!

Two chickens walk into a library, find the librarian and say, 'Buk BUK.' The librarian decides they want two books. She hands them over, and the chickens leave.

An hour later, the two chickens are back and looking annoyed. 'Buk Buk BuKKOOK' they say. The librarian decides the chickens want another three books, hands them over, and once again the chickens leave.

An hour later, the two birds march back in, looking very angry and shout, 'Buk Buk Buk Buk Bukkooook!'

The librarian is starting to get worried about where all her books are going. She decides to give the chickens more books but follow them and find out what's happening.

She follows them out of town and into a park. She hides behind a tree, not wanting to be seen. To her amazement, she sees the chickens showing the books to a frog who is saying, '*Rrredit Rrredit Rrredit...*'

What do you call a fish with no eyes?

A fsh.

What did the frog order at the restaurant?

French flies and a diet Croak.

Why are rhinos so wrinkly?

Because they're hard to iron.

Caller: I'm through at last! I've been trying to call the zoo for hours.

Zoo keeper: Yes, sorry, all our lions were busy.

What's a frog's favourite game in winter?

Ice hoppy.

What do you get when you cross a sheep and a frog?

A woolly jumper.

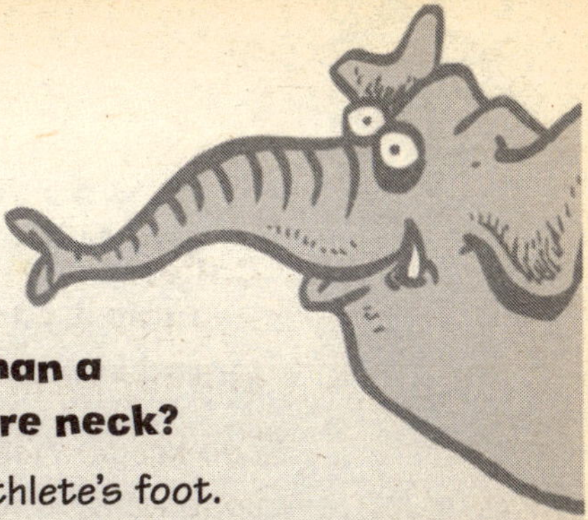

What is worse than a giraffe with a sore neck?

A centipede with athlete's foot.

Which side of a sheep has the most wool?

The outside.

What do you get when you cross a pig with a centipede?

Bacon and legs.

How do you know which end is a worm's face?

Tickle it and see which end laughs.

What breed of dog does a scientist own?

A lab.

What did the dolphin say to the whale when he swam into him?

Sorry, I didn't do it on porpoise.

A polar bear walks into a bar and says, 'I'll have a large orange juice . . . .

. . . .

. . . .

. . . .

. . . .

. . . .

. . .with ice.'

The bartender serves the juice and says: 'Here it is, but why the big pause?'

'I don't know,' the polar bear replied. 'I've always had them.'

How long should a reindeer's legs be?

Just long enough to reach the ground.

Why did the turkey cross the road?

Because it was spying on the chicken.

What did the polite mouse say?

'Cheese and thank you.'

What did the snake say to his girlfriend?

'C'mon, let's hiss and make up.'

How do you catch a rabbit?

Hide behind a tree and make carrot noises.

Why do bears have fur coats?

Because they'd look stupid in anoraks.

How do frogs die?

They Kermit suicide.

What country do cows love to visit?

Moo Zealand.

How many gorillas does it take to change a light bulb?

One, but it takes an awful lot of light bulbs.

Monstrous Mirth

How does a yeti get to work?

By icicle.

What do vampires eat for breakfast?

Dreaded Wheat.

What happened when the girl vampire met the boy vampire?

It was love at first bite.

How does a sorceress tell the time?

By looking at her witch watch.

What would you find on a haunted beach?

A sand witch.

What kinds of tests do they give witches?

Hex-ams.

What did the monster say to his girlfriend?

Hello gore-juice.

What is green and cross and goes around and around?

A witch stuck in a revolving door.

What happened when the monster met the young witch?

It was love at first fright.

First zombie: Meet my new girlfriend.
Second zombie: Wow! Where did you dig her up from?

What did the undertaker say to his girlfriend?

'I'm embalmy about you.'

What did the mother monster tell the baby monster when he ate too fast?

'Stop goblin your food.'

What's a mummy's favourite music?

Wrap music.

Who does a ghoul fall in love with?

His ghoul friend.

What do you call two witches that share a room?

Broom-mates.

What do you call a yeti in a phone box?

Stuck.

Which monster plays the most practical jokes?

Prankenstein.

Did you hear about the vampire who died of a broken heart?

He had loved in vein.

What kind of fur do you get from a werewolf?

As fur away as you can.

What's the best thing to do if a monster breaks down your front door?

Run out of the back door.

What's green and walks through walls?

Casper the Friendly Pickle.

What do you call a clever monster?

Frank Einstein.

What was the hippie vampire like?

He was ghoul, man. Real ghoul.

What is a zombie's favourite dessert?

Leeches and scream.

What do you do with a blue monster?

Try and cheer him up.

Did you hear about the sick werewolf?

He lost his voice but he's howl right now.

What do ghosts love to eat for breakfast?

Rice Creepies.

What's green, incredibly tall, and mopes in the corner?

The Incredible Sulk.

What's green, incredibly tall, and wrinkled?

The Incredible Sulk's granny.

What is a ghost's preferred food?

Spook-ghetti.

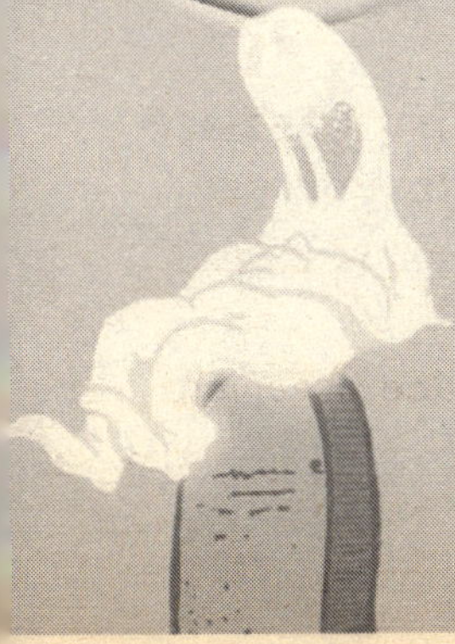

Knock,
Knock

Knock, knock.
Who's there?
Alex.
Alex who?
Alex plain later.

Knock,knock.
Who's there?
Cyril.
Cyril who?
Cyril pleasure to meet you again.

Knock, knock.

Who's there?

Dishes.

Dishes who?

Dishes a very bad joke.

Knock, knock.

Who's there?

Irene.

Irene who?

Irene and Irene but you still don't answer the door.

Knock, knock.
Who's there?
Oscar.
Oscar who?
Oscar silly question, you'll get a silly answer.

Knock, knock.
Who's there?
Yaa.
Yaa who?
What Yaa getting so excited about?

Knock, knock.

Who's there?

Danielle.

Danielle who?

Danielle at me, it's not my fault.

Knock, knock.

Who's there?

Fatso.

Fatso who?

Fatso funny about 'knock, knock' jokes?

Knock, knock.
Who's there?
Handsome.
Handsome who?
Handsome money through the keyhole and I'll tell you.

Knock, knock.
Who's there?
Viola.
Viola who?
Viola sudden don't you know me?

Knock, knock.
Who's there?
Rupert.
Rupert who?
Rupert your left arm in, your left arm out...

Knock, knock.
Who's there?
Mabel.
Mabel who?
Mabel doesn't ring either.

Knock, knock.
Who's there?
Luke.
Luke who?
Luke through the keyhole and you'll see.

Knock, knock.
Who's there?
Czech.
Czech who?
Czech before you open the door.

Knock, knock.

Who's there?

Major.

Major who?

Major answer, didn't I?

Knock, knock.

Who's there?

Obi Wan.

Obi Wan who?

Obi Wan of your friends. Let me in.

Knock, knock.
Who's there?
Chicken.
Chicken who?
Chicken your pockets, I think you've got my keys.

Knock, knock.
Who's there?
Gladys.
Gladys who?
Gladys my last joke?

Just Dumb!

What did the grape say when someone trod on it?

Nothing, it just gave a little whine.

How do you get 16 Pikachus on a bus?

You Pokémon.

Why don't you take a shower with a Pokémon?

He might take a Pikachu.

How do you make an egg laugh?

Tell it a yolk.

How do you throw
a party in space?

You planet!

What do you get if
you cross a lake with
a leaky boat?

About halfway.

What happened to the man who drowned in his muesli?

He was dragged under by a particularly strong currant.

What animal would you like to be on a cold day?

A little otter.

Did you hear the joke about the oak tree?

It's acorny one.

Why do they have a fence around the graveyard?

Because everyone is dying to get in.

Did you hear about the sunburnt shark?

He got what he was basking for.

What monkey can fly?

A hot-air baboon.

What did one volcano say to the other volcano?

I lava you.

What's small and cuddly and bright red?

A koala holding his breath.

What starts with T,
ends with T and
is full of T?

A teapot.

What did one
wall say to the
other wall?

**Meet you at the
corner.**

What did Captain Cook say to his men before they got on the ship?

'Let's get on the ship, men!'

What happened when a ship carrying red paint collided with a ship carrying blue paint?

Both crews were marooned.

Have you
heard the one about
the three holes
in the ground?

No.

Well, well, well.

Why did the orange go
to the doctor?

It wasn't peeling well.

How do you make a Mexican chilli?

Take him to the North Pole.

What's black when it's clean, and white when it's dirty?

A blackboard.

What's E.T. short for?

Because he has little legs!

What do you call a piece of wood that's doing nothing?

Bored!

Did you hear about the actor who fell through the floor?

It was just a stage he was going through.

Why are elephants large, grey, and wrinkled?

Because if they were small, white, and smooth they would be aspirins.

Insults

You're so dumb, you would fail a blood test.
I don't know what makes you so dumb but it really works.
You're so dumb, if you threw a rock at the ground you'd miss.

Brains aren't everything. In fact, in your case, they're nothing.
Don't let your mind wander – it's too small to be let out on its own.
I know ironing boards that have a higher IQ than you.

You are depriving some village somewhere of an idiot.
I bet your brain feels as good as new, considering you've never used it.
When they were giving out brains, you thought they said canes, and you said, 'I won't need one of those.'

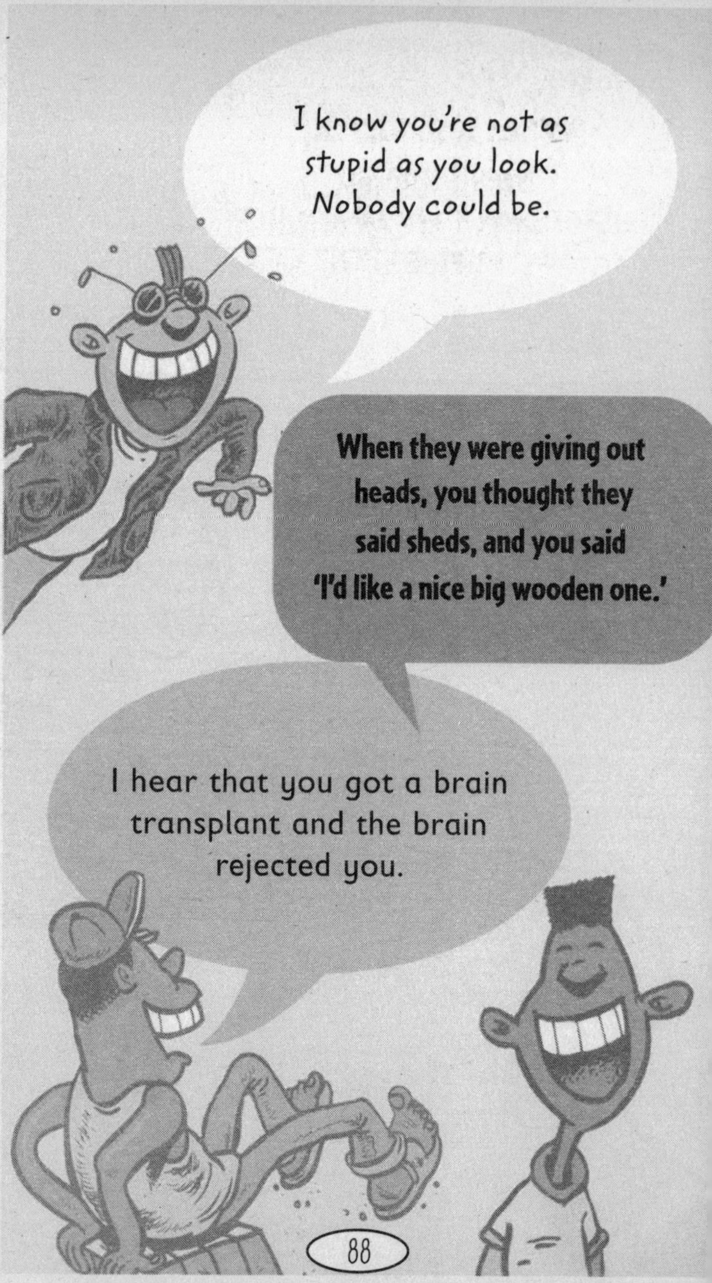
I know you're not as stupid as you look. Nobody could be.
When they were giving out heads, you thought they said sheds, and you said 'I'd like a nice big wooden one.'
I hear that you got a brain transplant and the brain rejected you.

What you lack in intelligence, you more than make up for in stupidity.
They didn't even give you an IQ, they knew you had no where to put it.
If you had an IQ of twelve you'd have to grow two more fingers to be able to count it.

So, a thought crossed your mind? Must have been a long and lonely journey.
Use your head. It's the little things that count.
I don't know what your exact IQ is, but it starts with a decimal point.

If your brain were chocolate, it wouldn't fill an M&M.
I thought of you all day today. I was at the zoo.
Everyone has the right to be ugly, but haven't you abused that privilege?

Don't you need a licence to be that ugly?
If I had a face like yours, I'd sue my parents.
I think you may have seen me at the zoo, I was the one feeding you peanuts.

When they were giving out noses, you thought they said roses, and you said, 'Give me a big red one.'
Is that your nose, or are you just eating a banana?
I see you were so impressed with your first chin that you added two more.

I've seen healthier looking faces on a pirate flag.
When you were born, you were so ugly, your mother didn't know which end to put the nappy on.
That isn't your forehead, it's your hair trying to run away from your face.

You're so ugly, that when you were born, the doctor smacked your mother.
You're so ugly that, when you were a baby, your parents fed you with a catapult.
When they were giving out looks, you thought they said books, and you said, 'Give me something funny'.

Over To You

New jokes are being created all the time, so we are constantly adding to our files to make sure we have all the best jokes around. If you or your friends hear any jokes that you really like, let us know about them. You can e-mail us at:
jokes@michaelomarabooks.com

We'll let you know if your jokes are going to be included in the next book.

Thanks.